French baking

SUE LAWRENCE

SIMON & SCHUSTER
A VIACOM COMPANY

First published in Great Britain by Martin Books, 1997
a division of Simon & Schuster
A Viacom Company

Martin Books, Grafton House, 64 Maids Causeway
Cambridge CB5 8DD

First published 1997
Copyright recipes and text © 1997 Le Creuset UK Limited
and Sue Lawrence
Copyright photographs © 1997 Le Creuset UK Limited

ISBN 0 85941 949 5

Design and typesetting: Jane Humphrey
Photography: Steve Baxter
Food stylist: Jane Stevenson
Styling: Roisin Nield

Printed and bound in Italy

Picture Credits: pages 8 and 50 Image Bank; pages 18, 28 and
38-9 Robert Harding Picture Library

Le Creuset UK Ltd
4 Stephenson Close
East Portway
Andover
Hants SP10 3RU

A Division of The Le Creuset Group

On the front cover: *Tarte aux Myrtilles, page 43*

CONTENTS

FOREWORD

Few things are so evocative of a particular place or time as the smell of freshly baked bread or cakes. The aroma of croissants and coffee conjures up misty Parisian streets early in the morning, while a sweet-pastry tart filled with dark, glistening 'myrtilles' reminds us of scented woods of the mountainous south. The taste of bread, cakes or tarts, just out of the oven, has to be among the greatest of culinary pleasures.

France, with its varieties of regional cuisine and its wonderful ingredients, can offer a multitude of such delicacies and is recognised as the home of pâtisserie in all its forms. France is also famed as the home of Le Creuset cast-iron cookware and the two are surprisingly compatible.

The northern French town of Fresnoy Le Grand is the home of Le Creuset; every single piece distributed worldwide is manufactured here. Each piece is made with the care and precision cooks have come to respect and enjoy.

The qualities of Le Creuset cast iron are well known: evenness of heating; good heat retention; energy efficiency and a smooth, vitreous enamel finish. These qualities make Le Creuset especially good for baking. Cakes and bread require even oven temperatures but the dish they are cooked in also plays a significant role in achieving a good result. When you bake in cast iron, the gentle spread of heat helps cakes and bread to rise and colour evenly, often at a lower temperature than you have to use for thinner baking tins, saving energy.

Even quite experienced cooks often steer clear of making home-made quiches, tarts and pies, because they fear the pastry base will be soggy and unappetising, however good the filling might be. This will be a worry of the past, if you make your recipe in one of the many round or oval gratin dishes. The secret is, again, in the properties of cast iron. The oven heat is transferred right to the centre of the dish, cooking the pastry to crisp, golden perfection, and the enamel surface will prevent the pastry from sticking to the dish.

As you read through this book, you will notice that dishes of other shapes can also make ideal baking dishes. A buffet casserole or skillet can be used to cook Tarte Tatin, a recipe which begins on the hob before being transferred to the oven. Many Le Creuset dishes have the flexibility to do this with no effort at all and, because Le Creuset is so colourful and attractive, you can cook quiches, tarts or pies and serve them straight to your table from the cooking dish.

So, open your cupboard door, look at your Le Creuset dishes in a new light and present your family and friends with baking and pâtisserie you will be remembered for.

Bon Appetit!
Le Creuset

INTRODUCTION

The art of baking and the art of cooking are like chalk and cheese. Whereas in cooking you can be wonderfully vague, throwing the entire contents of your fridge into salads, sauces, casseroles and soups, with baking you *must* be precise. Not only must you measure precisely but you must always time exactly – or certainly until you understand a little more about home-baking.

Having said that, there is no mystery about baking; it simply takes a little time to build up enough experience, by observing the 'behaviour' of your baking at every stage, to be confident that you understand what is happening in the bowl and in the baking tin.

Baking, by definition, involves the oven and it is crucial to get to know the idiosyncrasies of your own oven, as well as to understand the different heating techniques it uses for different settings, if it has them. For example, everyone knows that fan ovens should cook food on all shelves at the same temperature, whereas in conventional ovens, the top shelf will be hotter and the lower ones cooler than the middle shelf. Check your oven-manufacturer's handbook for information and recommendations and treat temperatures and timings in recipes as guidelines rather than infallible directives. Always remember that it is easier to remedy under-cooking than over-cooking.

Although many cakes and breads taste best just out of the oven, you can use your freezer to best advantage with most home-baking. Some cakes can even be fully iced, 'open-frozen' (uncovered) and then overwrapped and frozen for several weeks. For savoury

and sweet tarts, you can freeze at various stages: either freeze a ball of uncooked pastry; freeze the uncooked pastry rolled out into the prepared tart tin or freeze the pastry case after you have baked it blind. You can freeze many fruit-filled sweet tarts completely, once filled and baked. Savoury tarts, filled with a basic egg custard (whether it be made with milk, cream or crème fraîche) will lose their fresh, light texture in the freezer. For most savoury tarts, I would advise baking the pastry blind, freezing this and then filling and baking just before serving. If you are serving it for guests, you will have the added advantage of those evocative smells emanating from the oven.

I feel strongly that good food should not only taste (and smell) good, it should take up as little time as possible. So, if something can be done just as well in a food processor, I would always advise using it. I make all my pastry in the food processor, for general ease and speed. It is, however, extremely important to allow pastry to rest in a cool place – whether it is made by hand or by machine – before rolling it out. Then, once it is rolled out, leave it to rest again (preferably overnight), to prevent shrinkage. There are certain corners that simply cannot be cut. Similarly, when bread-making, you cannot speed up the rising and proving stages. If the dough rises too fast, it is likely to deflate in the oven. But most cakes and biscuits can be very quickly prepared and then baked at once.

Once you have followed the basic guidelines for baking and have become convinced that you will never again even consider a shop-bought cake or tart, you will also agree with me that there is absolutely nothing to compare with home-baking. The joy of mixing and kneading, the evocative smells, but most of all the taste, are satisfying, comforting and memorable.

During my four years of studying French at university, I spent many holidays in France. I also studied briefly at Caen University, was *au pair* in Arles in Provence and taught English, as an *assistante* in Lourdes, in the Pyrenees. In every region of France, I found the same attitude to food: passionate. Whether it was a *blanquette de veau* in the south-west, a *soupe à l'oignon* in Paris or a *tarte aux pommes* in Normandy, the cook and diner would both extol the virtues of the dish with a passion I had never seen at British tables. Animated discussions over the provenance of the meat, the variety of apple or the pungency of the garlic were commonplace and affected me greatly. During those years I learned that there was more to food than simply eating.

All these years later, I, too, find myself giving little homilies about the freshness of the fish, the ripeness of the cheese or the sweetness of the apples, so imbued was I in France with that passion and love for good food and all it stands for. There has never been any question about what Le Creuset has stood for. Ever since I was given my first Le Creuset saucepan, during my year living in France, I have realised that Le Creuset is synonymous with quality, durability and success; success not only on the hob but also in the oven, as you bake. Cakes, tarts, quiches and biscuits can all be reliably baked in Le Creuset. But don't take my word for it. Try for yourself.

Sue Lawrence, 1997

With special thanks to Sue Cutts, home economist for Le Creuset.

RECIPE NOTES: The oven temperatures and timings are for conventional ovens. For fan ovens, please consult the manufacturer's handbook.
All teaspoon and tablespoon measurements are level.
All eggs are medium unless otherwise stated.
Measurements are given in both metric and imperial units. Use either set of quantities, but not a mixture of both, in any one recipe.

AMERICAN AND AUSTRALIAN CONVERSION CHART

	BRITISH	AMERICAN	AUSTRALIAN
teaspoons and tablespoons	1 teaspoon	1 teaspoon	1 teaspoon
	1 tablespoon	1 rounded tablespoon	1 scant tablespoon
	2 tablespoons	2 tablespoons	1½ tablespoons
	3 tablespoons	3 tablespoons	2½ tablespoons
	4 tablespoons	4 tablespoons	3½ tablespoons
	5 tablespoons	5 tablespoons	4½ tablespoons
cup measures for liquids	4 tablespoons	¼ cup	¼ cup
	125 ml	½ cup	½ cup
	250 ml	1 cup	1 cup
	450 ml	2 cups	2 cups
	600 ml	2½ cups	2½ cups
cup measures for solids	225 g butter	1 cup	1 cup
	225 g caster sugar	1 cup	1 cup
	125 g icing sugar	1 cup	1 cup
	225 g flour	2 cups	2 cups
	175 g dried fruit	1 cup	1 cup
	225 g grated hard cheese, such as Parmesan	2 cups	2 cups
	60 g breadcrumbs	½ cup	½ cup
	200 g long-grain rice	1 cup	1 cup
	2 medium onions, chopped	1 cup	1 cup

BREADS

Bread is something I feel very strongly about. It was during my various stays in France that I realised there was more to bread than sliced or unsliced. At every single meal there was a fresh baguette, crusty and inviting. In the country, there was *pain de campagne*, simple, rustic and satisfying.

Thankfully, in Britain things have changed for the better and we have every sort of bread, from Italian, French or German to Californian sourdough, Lebanese and Indian. But there is still nothing quite as satisfying as the anticipation of tasting your own, home-made bread.

The even cooking and heat-retention of cast iron gives superb cooking results for many types of bread and you may, already, have a shape in your cupboard you could use. An oblong 22 cm (8½-inch) terrine dish can double as a 1 kg (2 lb) loaf tin and a pizza tray enables you to bake those wonderfully rustic flat breads to perfection. A bonus, if it were needed, is that cast iron will keep the bread deliciously warm at the table, so the freshly baked bread smells go on and on.

Flour is the principal ingredient in bread and so your home-made bread will only be as good as the flour you make it with. The best flours are the traditional stone-ground ones (the stone-grinding doesn't generate so much heat, which helps preserve the flavour of the grain).

There is a bit of mystique surrounding bread-making, but in fact it is a very straightforward process, once you understand the purpose of each stage. Yeast is added to bread to make it rise: most of these recipes use easy-blend yeast, which can just be added to the flour, without needing to be activated first. Kneading the dough helps it to develop an elastic smooth texture, which is necessary if it is to rise and not be heavy. The dough usually needs two 'resting' periods, during which time it can double in size. It's best to do this in a warm place such as a warm room or even the airing cupboard; the warmer the place, the swifter the rise. Don't overdo the heat, though, as yeast can be killed at very high temperatures and, if the dough rises too quickly, it may collapse in the oven.

The first period, called 'rising', takes place before the dough is shaped. Afterwards, punch the dough down with your fists, shape it and put in the loaf tin(s) if necessary and leave to 'prove' again.

When baking bread there isn't a visual test for when the loaf is done. Instead, tip the loaf out of the tin, if it's in a tin, and tap it with your knuckles on the base. It should sound hollow: if it doesn't, put the loaf back in the oven for another 5 minutes and then test again.

FOUGASSE AUX OLIVES

Makes 1 fougasse Freezing recommended
Preparation time: 30 minutes + about 4 hours rising + 25 minutes baking

Fougasse (also known as 'pompe') is a Provençal bread which, in its sweet form, is served on Christmas Eve, as the centrepiece of the traditional '13 Desserts' (representing the 12 disciples and Christ). But there are also savoury versions, made in the same shape, which are studded with olives or with Provençal herbs. The main characteristic is the shape: an oval, slashed with holes that open out as the bread bakes to look like the veins of a leaf. This is a lovely bread to serve for a casual supper, on a wooden board in the middle of the table, for guests to tear off chunks as required.

675 g (1 lb 8 oz) strong white bread flour
2 teaspoons salt
6 g (¼ oz) sachet easy-blend dried yeast
2 tablespoons olive oil
about 400 ml (14 fl oz) hand-hot water
12–16 black olives, stoned
coarse sea salt

1 Sift the flour and salt into a large bowl and stir in the yeast. Make a well in the centre and stir in the oil and sufficient water to form a stiff dough.

2 Turn on to a floured board and knead for about 10 minutes, until the dough feels smooth.

3 Place in a lightly oiled bowl and cover. Leave somewhere warm for about 1½–2 hours, until well risen.

4 Turn out the dough and knead very briefly again. Shape into a large oval. Place this on an oiled pizza or baking tray. Make 4 diagonal 'slits' on each side of the oval – as if you were drawing the veins of a leaf. Pull these slightly apart, so they do not close up during cooking. Top with the olives, pressing them in gently and then sprinkle over some sea salt.

5 Cover loosely with oiled cling film and leave to prove somewhere warm for about 1½ hours, or until slightly puffed up. Preheat the oven to Gas Mark 7/220°C/425°F.

6 Gently pull the slits apart once again and then bake until the loaf is golden brown and sounds hollow underneath when tapped (15–20 minutes if using a Le Creuset pizza tray, 20–25 minutes if using a baking tray). Transfer to a wire rack to cool.

PAIN AUX LARDONS

Makes 1 loaf Freezing recommended
Preparation time: 20 minutes + 2 hours rising + 20 minutes baking

Among the many rustic *pains de campagne* I enjoyed in the South of France, one of my favourites was *pain aux lardons* – bacon bread. In order to achieve a similar texture to French 'country' bread, I have substituted some strong wholemeal flour for some of the white. Serve this bread warm, with a bowl of vegetable soup in winter or a fresh, well tossed salad in summer.

150 g (5½ oz) strong wholemeal flour
350 g (12 oz) strong white flour
1 level teaspoon salt
6 g (¼ oz) sachet of easy-blend dried yeast
2 tablespoons olive oil
about 300 ml (½ pint) hand-hot water
125 g (4½ oz) streaky bacon

1 Place both flours in a large bowl and stir in the salt and yeast. Make a well in the centre.

2 Stir in the oil and the water and then combine with your hands to a dough.

3 Turn the dough on to a lightly floured board and knead for about 10 minutes, until smooth. Place in a lightly oiled bowl, cover and leave somewhere warm for about 1–1½ hours, until well risen.

4 Grill the bacon until crisp. Cut it into small pieces.

5 Tip the dough on to the floured board and knead in the bacon pieces, distributing them as evenly as you can.

6. Shape into an oblong with any joins underneath and place in a well oiled 22 cm (8½-inch), oblong terrine dish or in a 1 kg (2 lb) loaf tin.

7 Leave, loosely covered, somewhere warm, for about an hour. Preheat the oven to Gas Mark 7/220°C/425°F if using a Le Creuset terrine dish, Gas Mark 8/230°C/450°F if using a loaf tin.

8 Bake for about 20 minutes, or until the loaf is well risen and golden brown and sounds hollow when the base is tapped. Allow to cool for at least 30 minutes before cutting.

PAINS AUX RAISINS

Makes 12–15 Freezing recommended

Preparation time: 30 minutes + 2 hours rising + overnight proving + 15 minutes baking

Since *pains aux raisins* are a morning treat, I have given a recipe which involves overnight proving. There is nothing more satisfying than having a tray of freshly home-baked breads ready for breakfast. *Pains aux raisins* are ideal to make for weekend guests, for all the preparation can be done the day before. All you have to do on the morning is to switch on the oven while you casually make the morning tea. Then await those glorious home-baking aromas and the admiration of your guests. You are – just this once – allowed to look smug.

450 g (1 lb) strong white flour, sifted

2 x 6 g (¼oz) sachets of easy-blend dried yeast

1 teaspoon salt

25 g (1 oz) caster sugar

85 g (3 oz) unsalted butter, diced

250 ml (9 fl oz) hand-hot milk

FOR THE FILLING:

60 g (2 oz) unsalted butter, softened

60 g (2 oz) soft dark brown sugar

1 teaspoon ground cinnamon

125 g (4½ oz) raisins

½ egg, beaten, to glaze

1 Place the flour, dried yeast, salt and sugar in a large bowl. Rub in the butter, until the mixture resembles breadcrumbs. Make a well in the centre and pour in the milk, stirring well.

2 Gather together with your hands, to form a ball. Remove this to a lightly floured board and knead for about 10 minutes or until it feels smooth and elastic.

3 Place in a lightly oiled bowl, cover with cling film and leave to rise in a warm place (such as an airing cupboard) for at least 2 hours, by which time it should have risen to about 1½ times its original volume.

4 Roll out the dough to a rectangle, about 25 x 40 cm (10 x 16 inches). Spread all over with the softened butter and then combine the sugar and cinnamon and sprinkle evenly over the top. Scatter the raisins evenly over, and then carefully roll up, swiss-roll style, to form a long sausage.

5 Cut this into 12–15 slices and place these, cut-side up, on a buttered baking sheet or pizza tray. Cover loosely with buttered cling film and place in your fridge overnight.

6 Next morning, remove the baking sheet from the fridge to somewhere warm for 20 minutes, while you preheat the oven to Gas Mark 7/220°C/425°F.

7 Just before baking, glaze the tops with beaten egg, using a pastry brush. Bake for 12–15 minutes, or until golden brown.

8 Remove to a wire rack and devour while still warm.

BRIOCHE

Makes 1 brioche Freezing recommended
Preparation time: 20 minutes + 14 hours resting + 40 minutes baking

Because brioche contains very little yeast and lots of butter, it takes a long time to produce, from start to finish. Unlike most yeast-based breads, which require one long rising then a shorter proving, brioche generally needs three resting periods altogether. Although I have given approximate times for these, the process can, of course, be hurried along somewhat by placing the dough somewhere warm. I would recommend leaving it at room temperature, however, in order to achieve a light, finely crumbed texture. If the dough rises too quickly, the texture tends to be looser and rather more 'holey'.

Serve slices of brioche warm as a pudding, with fruit compote; or cold, for breakfast with good butter and a lovely, runny French conserve.

Although I have tried making brioche with dried yeast, I do prefer using fresh yeast for it: buy in bulk and freeze in small portions.

15 g (½ oz) fresh yeast
85 ml (3 fl oz) hand-hot milk
450 g (1 lb) strong white flour
1 teaspoon salt
25 g (1 oz) caster sugar
175 g (6 oz) unsalted butter, softened
3 eggs, beaten
beaten egg to glaze

1 Mash the yeast into the warm milk and leave for 5 minutes.

2 Sift the flour into a large mixing bowl and then add the salt and sugar. Make a well in the centre. Pour in the eggs and beat well.

3 Scoop off small pieces of the softened butter with your fingers and incorporate these gradually into the mixture, rubbing and squeezing the butter into the flour. Gather the dough together with your hands and turn on to a floured board. Knead for 4–5 minutes. Put the dough in an oiled bowl and cover. Leave at room temperature for about 3 hours.

4 Turn on to a floured board and then knead the dough for a further 2–3 minutes. Return to the bowl and cover. Place in the fridge and leave for at least 8 hours, or overnight.

5 Turn the dough on to a floured board and divide it into two pieces: one-third and two-thirds. Roll the larger piece into the shape of a ball and place this in a buttered 1.2 litre (2-pint) brioche mould. Roll the smaller piece into a ball and place it on top. Press down gently and then lightly brush with beaten egg. Save the remaining egg.

6 Cover loosely with oiled cling film and leave at room temperature for about 3 hours or until well risen. Preheat the oven to Gas Mark 7/220°C/425°F.

7 Glaze once again with beaten egg and then snip about five little cuts around the edge with kitchen scissors, to give the classic 'bubbled' edges. Bake for 20 minutes. Lower the heat to Gas Mark 5/190°C/375°F and bake for a further 15–20 minutes. Cover the brioche loosely with foil towards the end, so it does not burn. Remove from the mould to cool on a wire rack.

PECHES JAUNES DE PROVENCE
LE KG 9F80
MELON DE CAVAILLON "COCCINELLE"
LE KG 24F
NECTARINE DU ROUSSILLON
LE KG 9F80
FEVES
LE KG 14F
FIGUES 24
CAVAILLON "COCCINELLE"
LE KG 24F
LA PIECE
COURGETTE 6F
CAVAILLON
LA PIECE 9F

SAVOURY TARTS

I have always loved eating local savoury pastries, wherever I have travelled. I remember flaky cheese pastries, eaten in a boat crossing the Aegean Sea, hearty meat-filled pies in the bustling streets of Caracas and neat little *pirozhki* (cabbage-filled patties) in a blizzard-ridden Moscow.

The most pleasant memories – for me anyway – always involve sunshine, and so the savoury tarts of France fill me with joy. Their tomato, onion and ratatouille tarts evoke sunshine, instantly. Even the ubiquitous – and much adulterated – quiche Lorraine, when properly executed, can be truly memorable.

With savoury tarts, the pastry is every bit as important as the filling, which is why I have given different pastry recipes for each tart. Mix and match as you try the various combinations: I do this all the time.

The advantage of using a cast-iron dish for pastry is that soft, undercooked pastry bases can be a thing of the past.

Pastry cooked in cast iron will be dry, crisp and golden, both over the top and underneath. There is no need to grease the dish: the very smooth enamel surface ensures the pastry won't stick.

Round or oval, large or small, there are a variety of gratin-dish shapes you can use, including egg plates: small dishes that have a variety of uses and make delightful small sweet or savoury tarts. Perhaps there is an under-used gratin dish lurking in your cupboard; if so, now is the time to put it to greater use by baking a delicious treat.

PISSALADIÈRE

Serves 6 Freezing not recommended

Preparation time: making + chilling pastry + 30 minutes cooking + 40 minutes baking

This is not the usual *pissaladière* you will find in Provence. There, it has more in common with a pizza than with a tart; it has a bread base and is usually topped with a thin layer of dense tomato sauce, some salt-cured black olives and anchovies. The classic *pissaladière*, however, was traditionally covered with *pissalat* (hence the name of the tart), which is made by rubbing through a sieve the young 'fry' of fish such as anchovies, which were previously pickled in brine for eight days. This purée was then diluted with some of the brine, spiced with cloves and decanted into airtight jars. Nowadays – thankfully – anchovies tend to be substituted for this rather pungent paste. I prefer to use a shortcrust pastry base for my recipe but I make the tart in a 'free-form' style, to retain its rustic good looks.

FOR THE PASTRY:

250 g (9 oz) plain flour, sifted

½ teaspoon salt

125 g (4½ oz) unsalted butter, diced

1 egg yolk

2–3 tablespoons cold water

FOR THE TOPPING:

3 tablespoons olive oil

1 large onion, chopped

2 large garlic cloves, chopped

400 g (14 oz) can of chopped tomatoes

2 tablespoons red wine

1 tablespoon chopped fresh marjoram plus 1 sprig

50 g (1¾ oz) Parmesan cheese, grated

50 g (1¾ oz) can of anchovies, drained

10–12 black olives, stoned

salt and freshly ground black pepper

1 For the pastry, first place the flour, salt and butter in a food processor and process to fine crumbs. Mix together the yolk and 2 tablespoons of water and pour them in, while the processor is running. Add just enough extra water to make it look moist. Gather the dough together with your hands and wrap in cling film. Chill for at least an hour.

2 Meanwhile, make the topping: heat the oil in a saucepan and gently fry the onion and garlic for about 10 minutes, until softened. Add the tomatoes (and their juice) and the wine and cook, uncovered, over a medium heat, for about 20 minutes, until it has thickened. Remove from the heat and add the marjoram and plenty of salt and pepper. Allow to cool.

3 Roll out to fit a 32 cm (12½-inch) pizza dish, pushing it into the edges to form a narrow rim. Prick all over and chill the base for at least an hour. Preheat the oven to Gas Mark 6/200°C/400°F.

4 Sprinkle the Parmesan over the pastry base. Top with the tomato sauce, smoothing out evenly. (It will be fairly chunky still – remember, this is a rustic tart.) Top with the anchovy fillets and dot with the black olives. Tear over the remaining marjoram leaves.

5 Bake for about 40 minutes, until the edges are golden brown and crisp. Leave to cool for at least 20 minutes before cutting and serving warm.

REBLOCHON AND BACON TART

Serves 6 Freezing not recommended
Preparation time: making + chilling pastry + 20 minutes + 50 minutes baking

I have always loved reblochon, that most wonderfully rich, soft and creamy cheese from Savoy. Although I have never eaten it in a cooked dish in France, I decided to start fiddling with it when I overdid the ordering and ended up with far too much left over after a party. The result is this tart, which – in my humble opinion – tastes really rather good, and definitely worth ordering extra reblochon for! Serve warm, with a green salad.

FOR THE PASTRY:

150 g (5½ oz) plain flour, sifted
½ teaspoon salt
75 g (2¾ oz) unsalted butter
1 small egg
2 teaspoons olive oil

FOR THE FILLING:

125 g (4½ oz) streaky bacon, chopped
250 g (9 oz) reblochon cheese
3 eggs
200 ml (7 fl oz) crème fraîche
salt and freshly ground black pepper

1 For the pastry, place the flour, salt and butter in a food processor. Whizz until the mixture resembles breadcrumbs. Mix together the egg and olive oil and add them through the feeder tube. Whizz briefly and then gather together with your hands. Wrap in cling film and chill for at least an hour.

2 Bring the pastry back to room temperature and roll out slightly larger than a 24 cm (9½-inch), oval gratin dish or a 22 cm (8½-inch), buttered, loose-bottomed tart tin. Place the pastry in the dish or tin. Prick the base all over and chill for at least 2 hours or, preferably, overnight. Preheat the oven to Gas Mark 5/190°C/375°F.

3 Line the tart with foil or greaseproof paper and fill it with baking beans. Bake blind for 12–15 minutes. Remove the beans and foil and cook for a further 5 minutes. Reduce the oven heat to Gas Mark 4/180°C/350°F.

4 For the filling, fry the bacon in its own fat, until crisp. Drain on kitchen paper.

5 Cut the rind off the cheese and cut the cheese into small pieces. Place the bacon and cheese on the base of the tart. Whisk together the crème fraîche and eggs and season with plenty of salt and pepper. Pour this over the base, spreading out evenly.

6 Bake for about 30 minutes, until the filling is puffed up and golden brown. Remove and allow to cool for about 15 minutes. Serve warm.

TOMATO AND MUSTARD TART

Serves 6 Freezing not recommended
Preparation time: making + chilling pastry + 1 hour baking

Here is a common dilemma. You're sitting at a polite dinner party, eating the most divine dish you've had in months. Do you ask the host or hostess for the recipe? Will they be flattered or will their response be more of a 'certainly not, it's mine and I'm not sharing it!'. I'm afraid I do not even consider the possibility of receiving a hostile response: I just plough in and ask for the recipe. When it is a friend you are asking, it is all the easier, of course!

The recipe below is the result of such an occasion. When Joanna Blythman, Britain's leading investigative food journalist, served her tomato and mustard tart for me, I was smitten. Joanna's recipe is a variation on one she was served by a friend on a summer's day in her garden, north of Lyons, when she used to live in France. She then changed it by adding a mixture of goat's cheese and Comté, and drizzling over some basil oil at the very end. I have altered it a little further, by adding some polenta to the flour, to give the pastry more crunch.

FOR THE PASTRY:
150 g (5½ oz) plain flour
½ teaspoon salt
50 g (1¾ oz) fine polenta
85 g (3 oz) unsalted butter, chilled and diced
1 egg, beaten
¾–1 tablespoon olive oil

FOR THE FILLING:
2 tablespoons Dijon mustard
100 g (3½ oz) goat's cheese (chèvre), diced
75 g (2¾ oz) gruyère cheese, grated

500 g (1 lb 2 oz) vine-ripened tomatoes
3 tablespoons olive oil
a handful of fresh basil leaves
salt and freshly ground black pepper

1 For the pastry, sift the flour and salt into a food processor and then add the polenta and butter. Process briefly, until the mixture resembles breadcrumbs. Then add the egg and just enough oil to form a moist dough, which can be gathered together in your hands to form a ball. Wrap in cling film and chill for at least 20 minutes.

2 Bring the pastry back to room temperature and roll out to fit a buttered 24 cm (9½-inch), loose-bottomed metal tart tin. Prick the base several times. Chill for at least 30 minutes. Preheat the oven to Gas Mark 6/200°C/400°F.

3 Spread the mustard evenly over the base and then top with the two cheeses. Cut the tomatoes into thick slices and lay them on top, in tight, overlapping circles, so the tomatoes sit up, slightly proud. Season generously. Drizzle over a tablespoon of olive oil.

4 Bake for 45 minutes, or until the pastry looks crisp at the edges and the tomatoes are beginning to caramelise.

5 Meanwhile, process the basil with 2 tablespoons of oil in a blender or processor, until you have a purée. (You might require extra oil if your processor bowl is large.)

6 Remove the tart from the oven and drizzle the basil oil all over the top. Turn off the oven, replace the tart and leave it in the oven for at least 15 minutes. Remove and allow to cool for at least 15 minutes before eating warm.

GRILLED PEPPER TARTLETS

Serves 6 Freezing not recommended
Preparation time: making + chilling pastry + grilling peppers + 45 minutes baking

These tartlets are one of my great favourites, as I love this short, cheesy pastry and the summery taste of grilled peppers. They also look fabulous, with the red-pepper slivers arranged like a lattice. You can also make one 24 cm (9½-inch) tart in a loose-bottomed tart tin, arranging the pepper slivers like the spokes of a wheel; you will have some pastry left over but it can be frozen.

FOR THE PASTRY:

225 g (8 oz) plain flour, sifted
¾ teaspoon salt
25 g (1 oz) Parmesan cheese, grated
140 g (5 oz) unsalted butter, chilled and diced
1 egg
1 tablespoon olive oil

FOR THE FILLING:

2 red peppers
300 ml (½ pint) double cream
2 eggs
50 g (1¾ oz) Parmesan cheese, grated
salt and freshly ground black pepper

1 For the pastry, place the flour, salt, Parmesan and butter in a food processor. Process until the mixture resembles breadcrumbs. Slowly add the egg, mixed with the oil, through the feeder tube, until the mixture forms a ball. Wrap in cling film and refrigerate for at least an hour.

2 For the filling, cut the peppers into quarters and remove the seeds. Place on a sheet of foil, under a hot grill. Grill until charred and blackened. Remove and wrap tightly in the foil. After about 20 minutes – or whenever they are cool enough to handle – remove and peel off the skins. Cut into slivers.

3 Bring the pastry back to room temperature and roll out to fit four Le Creuset egg plates or 16 cm (6½-inch) tartlet tins. Prick the bases and chill for at least an hour or, preferably, overnight.

4 Preheat the oven to Gas Mark 5/190°C/375°F. Line the tartlets with foil or greaseproof paper and fill them with baking beans. Bake blind for 10 minutes (15 minutes for tartlet tins). Remove the beans and foil or greaseproof paper. Cook for a further 5 minutes. Allow the tartlets to cool slightly. Reduce the oven heat to Gas Mark 3/160°C/325°F.

5 Arrange the slivers of pepper in the pastry cases. Whisk together the cream, eggs, Parmesan and plenty of salt and pepper. Pour carefully over the peppers.

6 Bake for about 15 minutes, until the filling is puffed up and golden brown. Allow to cool for at least 15 minutes before eating warm.

GOAT'S CHEESE AND ARTICHOKE TART

Serves 8 Freezing not recommended
Preparation time: making + chilling pastry + 10 minutes + 45 minutes baking

I love the strong, earthy taste of goat's cheese. This tart combines goat's cheese with artichokes, and makes a delicious and unusual dinner-party starter or a main course for lunch, with fresh green salad. Try to find artichoke hearts which have been marinated in extra virgin olive oil – not a mixture of sunflower and olive oils – and then you can use this oil for cooking, such as a salad dressing or pasta sauces.

FOR THE PASTRY:

150 g (5½ oz) plain flour, sifted
25 g (1 oz) fine oatmeal
½ teaspoon salt
100 g (3½ oz) unsalted butter, chilled and diced
1 egg, beaten
2 teaspoons olive oil

FOR THE FILLING:

200 g (7 oz) medium-strength goat's cheese (chèvre)
200 ml (7 fl oz) crème fraîche
3 eggs
290 g jar of artichoke hearts marinated in oil
salt and freshly ground black pepper

1 For the pastry, place the flour, oatmeal, salt and butter in a food processor and process until the mixture resembles breadcrumbs. Mix the egg and oil and then slowly add them, through the feeder tube. Gather the dough together with your hands and wrap it in cling film. Chill for at least an hour.

2 Bring the pastry back to room temperature. Roll out to fit a 22 cm (8½-inch), round gratin dish or a buttered, deep, 24 cm (9½-inch), loose-bottomed tart tin. Prick the base and chill for 1–2 hours or, preferably, overnight.

3 Preheat the oven to Gas Mark 5/190°C/375°F if using a Le Creuset gratin dish, Gas Mark 6/200°C/400°F if using a tart tin. Line the tart with foil or greaseproof paper and fill it with baking beans. Bake the pastry blind for 15 minutes. Remove the foil and beans and continue to bake for 5 minutes. Remove the tart and reduce the oven heat to Gas Mark 3/160°C/325°F if using a Le Creuset gratin dish, Gas Mark 4/180°C/350°F if using a tart tin.

4 For the filling, chop the goat's cheese and place it in a food processor or liquidiser, with the crème fraîche, eggs and plenty of salt and pepper. Whizz until well blended.

5 Drain the oil from the artichoke hearts and roughly chop the artichokes. Place these on the base of the tart and then pour over the goat's-cheese mixture. Bake for about 20–30 minutes if using a gratin dish or 30–40 minutes if using a tart tin, until the filling is puffed up and golden brown. Leave to cool for at least 20 minutes, before serving warm.

CAKES

According to some estate agents, if you really want to sell your house, bake a cake. The inviting aroma of a cake fresh from the oven is apparently enough to make even the strongest-willed among us surrender. It is indeed a comforting smell, which, with luck, is matched by the delicious taste.

Here are a few of my favourite French cakes, which are all very easy to do. Even the Buche de Noël (which you roll up like a roulade or swiss roll) can be made by children, as any mistakes can be patched up with the thick chocolate coating.

The lightest of sponge cakes, such as a Genoese sponge, can be baked in a cast-iron dish. The 30 cm (12-inch) rectangular dish is an ideal shape for sponge or fruit cakes and is especially good when you are cooking for a crowd. Lining the dish is not essential but, for larger cakes, lining does make handling much easier when the cake is hot.

Oven temperatures can, generally, be lower when baking in cast iron: as a simple guide, use two settings lower than your recipe suggests.

Judging when cakes are properly cooked is an important art in home-baking. Test heavy fruit cakes with a long skewer; if it comes out clean, the cake is done. For lighter sponge cakes, simply press lightly with your fingertips; if the cake feels springy, it is done.

Errors are, usually, reparable. If you feel you have taken your cake out of the oven too soon, simply pop it back in for a few minutes. If it's too late for that, cut the cake in wedges, warm it through and serve as a hot pudding, with cream.

It's a lot easier to remedy under-cooking than over-cooking, however, so always check a little before the end of the recommended cooking time. If the top is browning well before the middle is cooked, cover the cake with foil loosely, to protect it.

GÂTEAU AU CHOCOLAT

Serves 8–10 Freezing recommended
Preparation time: 20 minutes + 25 minutes baking

My friend Sabine, who lived in the Pyrenees during my teaching year at the Lourdes Lycée, used to invite me to her beautiful old house regularly, to feed me. On occasions, she would pop round to my tiny little flat with a freshly baked quiche or tart. On one occasion, when I had overdone the sun on a Sunday hill-walk (only a sun-starved Anglo-Saxon would lie, prostrate, on top of a mountain summit in the midday sun), she brought me treats for the two days I was confined inside with sun-stroke. One of those treats was a chocolate cake, which arrived fresh and still warm. The sensible French serve this type of rich chocolate cake in thin slivers, at the end of a dinner or lunch. I confess I ate rather more than the customary sliver. But it was medicinal, after all.

Back in freezing-cold Britain, I like to serve the cake warm, with crème fraîche or whipped cream and some fresh raspberries on the side.

150 g (5½ oz) dark chocolate (minimum 55%
cocoa solids)
1 tablespoon strong, black coffee
75 g (2¾ oz) caster sugar
75 g (2¾ oz) unsalted butter, softened
3 eggs, separated
100 g (3½ oz) plain flour, sifted
½ teaspoon baking powder

1 Preheat the oven to Gas Mark 4/180°C/350°F if using a Le Creuset gratin dish, Gas Mark 6/200°C/400°F if using a loose-bottomed cake tin. Melt the chocolate and coffee together in a bowl over a pan of gently simmering water. The water shouldn't touch the bottom of the bowl.

2 Add the sugar and butter and stir until it is all well combined and the butter has melted into the mixture.

3 Add the egg yolks and stir well. Sift in the flour and the baking powder and stir well.

4 Whisk the egg whites until they are stiff and then stir one large spoonful into the mixture, to lighten it. Once that is incorporated, gently fold in the remaining egg whites until thoroughly combined.

5 Pour the mixture into a paper-lined, heart-shaped gratin dish or a 20 cm (8-inch), buttered and lined, loose-bottomed cake tin. Level the surface.

6 Bake for 20–25 minutes, or until a fine skewer inserted into the middle comes out clean.

7 Place on a wire rack and leave to cool for 5 minutes before turning out. Allow to cool for at least 30 minutes, before cutting and serving warm, with crème fraîche or whipped cream and some raspberries.

GÂTEAU AU YAOURT

Serves 10 Freezing recommended
Preparation time: 15 minutes + 45 minutes baking

During my summer in Provence, as *au pair* to two little girls, I was introduced to many different tastes and flavours. I had my first taste of aubergines, courgettes, basil, fresh figs, rabbit and veal. I loved them all, but – as a sweet-toothed Scot – I did, occasionally, crave sweet things. The good people of Provence are not known for their home-baking expertise. There is simply no call for a slice of cake or a piece of shortbread with a warming cup of tea under the Mediterranean sun. So, when my two charges asked if they could bake a cake with me one day, I was thrilled. It was their very own recipe and I was amazed – not to say a trifle bemused – at their measuring techniques. Admittedly it was a yogurt cake, but absolutely everything was measured out in the cleaned yogurt pot. I thought this was peculiar to the little girls in Provence but I found yogurt cakes made in both the south-west and north-west of France in a similar way. They might be extravagant with their ingredients but the French can be economical with the washing-up! The texture of this cake is very moist, rather dense and worryingly moreish. The flavour of the rum comes through loud and clear, which makes me wonder about the taste-buds of my innocent little charges!

250 ml (9 fl oz) natural yogurt
2 eggs, beaten
350 g (12 oz) caster sugar
200 g (7 oz) self-raising flour, sifted
½ teaspoon baking powder
75 g (2¾ oz) desiccated coconut
1 tablespoon dark rum
50 ml (2 fl oz) extra virgin olive oil

1 Place everything together in a mixing bowl and, using a wooden spoon, stir everything together until well mixed.

2 Spoon into a buttered and lined 22 cm (8½-inch) oblong terrine or a 1 kg (2 lb) loaf tin and smooth the top.

3 Bake for 15 minutes at Gas Mark 3/160°C/325°F if using a Le Creuset terrine or Gas Mark 5/190°C/375°F if using a loaf tin. Then lower the heat to Gas Mark 2/150°C/300°F for a Le Creuset terrine or Gas Mark 3/160°C/325°F for a loaf tin and continue baking; a cake in a terrine will take 25–30 minutes, one in a loaf tin will take 40 minutes. Cover the cake very loosely with foil halfway through the baking time. Remove from the oven and leave to cool completely before turning out.

NORMANDY APPLE CAKE

Serves 8 Freezing not recommended
Preparation time: 15 minutes + 45 minutes baking

This is a cake that I enjoyed on a trip to Normandy. In fact, everywhere I went during a five-day trip, I was treated to a Normandy apple cake or tart. The following recipe is the one I loved most of all. Add a splash of Calvados to the batter just before baking, to add a true flavour of Normandy.

200 g (7 oz) caster sugar
4 eggs
300 ml (½ pint) crème fraîche
150 g (5½ oz) plain flour, sifted
750 g (1 lb 10 oz) cooking apples, peeled,
    cored and grated or diced small
75 g (2¾ oz) raisins
100 g (3½oz) butter, melted
a little Calvados (optional)

1 Preheat the oven to Gas Mark 3/160°C/325°F. Place the sugar and eggs in a bowl and whisk together.
2 Add the crème fraîche and flour and stir well.
3 Dry the apples and then add them to the bowl, with the raisins and melted butter. Add the Calvados, if using. Stir well to combine.
4 Spoon into a paper-lined, 30 cm (12-inch), rectangular baking dish or a cake tin measuring approximately 28 x 20 x 4 cm (11 x 8 x 1½ inches). Don't bother to smooth the surface – it will be rather bumpy with the apples.
5 Bake for 40–45 minutes, until the apples are tender and the batter is golden brown.
6 Allow to cool for at least 20 minutes in the dish and then serve warm, in slices.

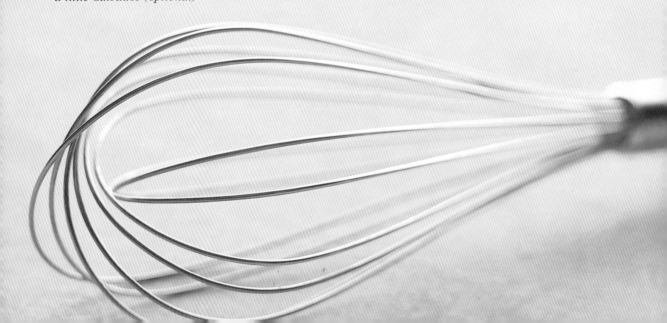

BÛCHE DE NOËL

Serves 8 Freezing recommended

Preparation time: 1 hour 15 minutes + 12 minutes baking + cooling + chilling

This is an ideal alternative dessert to produce on Christmas Day, with the Christmas pudding. It not only tastes divine, it looks fabulous. The marvellous thing about this chocolate log or *buche* is that it really does not matter if it cracks as you roll it up. You cover it with thick chocolate icing, so imperfections cannot be seen at all. This is a good cake to involve the children in, before Christmas. They not only love spreading the icing on to the log, they also love licking the bowl. So if, like me, you too are a closet bowl-licker, do this yourself while they are at school!

6 eggs, separated
150 g (5½ oz) caster sugar
250 g (9 oz) plain chocolate (minimum 55% cocoa solids)
4 tablespoons cold water
FOR THE ICING:
250 g (9 oz) unsalted butter, softened
450 g (1 lb) icing sugar, plus extra, to decorate
50 g (1¼ oz) cocoa powder
2 tablespoons milk

1 Preheat the oven to Gas Mark 7/220°C/425°F. Line a swiss-roll tin (23 x 33 cm/9 x 13 inches) with grease-proof paper and brush the paper with oil. Whisk the egg yolks and caster sugar together until light and thick.

2 Melt the chocolate and water in a bowl over gently simmering water, which should not touch the bottom of the bowl. Stir until smooth. Stir the egg mixture into the chocolate.

3 Whisk the egg whites until stiff but not dry. Gently fold a spoonful of the egg whites into the chocolate mixture, to lighten it. Then fold in the remaining egg whites, using a large metal spoon. Take care not to over mix. Pour the batter into the prepared swiss-roll tin.

4 Bake for 12–13 minutes, until puffed up and firm to the touch.

5 Remove and allow to cool completely, for at least 2 hours and, preferably, overnight.

6 For the icing, beat the butter until creamy. Sift in the icing sugar and cocoa. Add the milk and stir well until thoroughly combined.

7 Lay a sheet of greaseproof paper on your working surface and sprinkle it generously with sugar. With one bold movement, turn the whole cake on to the sheet of paper and then remove the tin. Carefully pull off the lining paper, which is now on top. Trim away any scraggy ends.

8 Spread half the icing over the cake, right to the edges.

9 Roll up as you would a swiss roll: starting at the long side opposite you, use the greaseproof paper to roll the cake towards you, around the icing. Don't worry about the cracks. Transfer to your serving plate. Chill for 20 minutes or so.

10 Carefully spread the remaining icing over the cake: you can pipe this, if you like, or simply spread it in neat strokes. Once all the icing has been used, swirl a little over the ends. Chill briefly, and then sift some icing sugar over the log.

SWEET TARTS

I rate a sweet tart (filled with fruit, nuts or, of course, chocolate) as one of my three all-time favourite desserts. The following tarts are all inspired by those I tasted and enjoyed in France. Although I give a basic sweet pastry recipe (page 63), I like to vary it by adding some ground nuts (usually almonds, but hazelnuts and walnuts are also good) and, sometimes, some lemon zest.

Sweet tarts serve a two-fold purpose: served slightly warm, with a dollop of cream or crème fraîche, they make superb desserts. Served cold, they make afternoon tea into a very special treat.

By the way, my other two favourite desserts are home-made ice cream and steamed puddings!

TARTE AUX PIGNONS

Serves 6–8 Freezing recommended
Preparation time: making pastry + chilling + 55 minutes baking

Pine kernels are used in many Provençal dishes. Often referred to by their Italian name *pignoli* in Provence, they are used in both savoury and sweet recipes. Their delicious creamy, nutty taste enhances this rich tart beautifully. I like to serve it barely warm with some tangy Greek yogurt, to cut through the sweetness of the tart.

FOR THE PASTRY:
125 g (4½ oz) plain flour, sifted
a pinch of salt
25 g (1 oz) caster sugar
50 g (1¾ oz) ground almonds
85 g (3 oz) unsalted butter, chilled and diced
1 egg yolk
1–2 tablespoons freshly squeezed lemon juice
FOR THE FILLING:
100 g (3½ oz) unsalted butter, melted
50 g (1¾ oz) light muscovado sugar
3 tablespoons golden syrup
1 tablespoon lemon juice
3 eggs, beaten
150 g (5½ oz) pine kernels

1 For the pastry, place the first four ingredients in a food processor and process briefly. Then add the butter and process until the mixture resembles breadcrumbs. Slowly add the yolk and just enough lemon juice to combine to a fairly moist dough. Gather the dough together with your hands and wrap in cling film. Chill for about an hour.

2 Bring back to room temperature and roll out to a circle a little larger than your buttered 20 cm (8-inch), loose-bottomed metal tart tin and place the pastry in the tin. Prick all over the base and then chill for at least 2 hours (preferably overnight).

3 Preheat the oven to Gas Mark 6/200°C/400°F. Line the pastry case with foil or greaseproof paper and fill with baking beans. Bake blind for 15 minutes. Then remove the foil and beans and bake for a further 5–10 minutes, until the pastry is almost cooked through. Lower the oven heat to Gas Mark 4/180°C/350°F.

4 For the filling, place the melted butter in a bowl and add all the other filling ingredients, apart from the pine kernels. Whisk together thoroughly. Sprinkle the pine kernels over the tart base and then pour over the butter mixture.

5 Bake for about 35 minutes or until the filling is set and is a deep golden colour. Allow to cool for at least 45 minutes before cutting.

TARTE AUX MYRTILLES

Makes 1 large tart, serves 8 Freezing recommended
Preparation time: making + chilling pastry + 15 minutes + 40 minutes baking

During one of my university vacations, I was *au pair* in Provence for a young family. The family's holiday was in the French Pyrenees, where they had a rickety old house perched on a cliff-side in a tiny mountain village. Most days were spent driving into the forests and woods to pick *myrtilles* – the native bilberries. As we drove slowly along the mountain tracks, there would suddenly be a cry of *myrtilles* from the back as the children had spotted some under the trees. Everyone then hurtled out from the car to gather as many of those wonderfully sweet berries as possible. Those which were not immediately consumed were incorporated into the most wonderful jams and tarts. Since Madame Zelt did not have anything as sophisticated as a proper tart tin in the ramshackle kitchen, she improvised by making a 'free-style' tart on a baking sheet; I have based my recipe on this. Since bilberries are difficult to find in Britain, I suggest substituting blueberries, which are available all year round.

1 quantity of sweet shortcrust pastry (page 63), chilled
600 g (1 lb 5 oz) blueberries
50 g (1¾ oz) caster sugar
1 heaped tablespoon semolina
egg white and caster sugar, to glaze

1 Preheat the oven to Gas Mark 6/200°C/400°F. Roll out the chilled pastry to a circle, about 6 cm (2½ inches) wider than the pizza tray, which is about 32 cm (12½ inches) wide.

2 Lift the pastry carefully on to the pizza tray.

3 Combine the berries with the sugar and semolina, ensuring you do this gently, so the berries are not bruised.

4 Pile the berries in the centre of the pastry and then fold in the edges: turn the pastry in, to form a wide crust all round. You should have a circle of berries showing in the middle.

5 Using a pastry brush, brush all over the crust with egg white and then sprinkle with some caster sugar.

6 Bake for about 40 minutes or until the pastry is golden brown and the berries are oozing and juicy. Remove from the oven and allow to cool for at least 20 minutes before cutting.

TARTE TATIN

Makes 1 tart, serves 8 Freezing not recommended
Preparation time: making + chilling pastry + 30 minutes + 35 minutes baking

There is something deeply satisfying about a tarte tatin. It is a combination of the appearance – so sticky and inviting – and the smell, of caramelised apples and buttery pastry, which is so evocative. Finally, there is the unashamed pride of the cook, having managed to invert it – all in one piece – on to the serving plate! It is in fact incredibly easy to invert, as there is plenty of butter to help it slide out. But, should any recalcitrant bits stick to the pan, they can all be easily patched up. You need to use a pan that can first go on the hob and then be transferred to the oven. I use a 26 cm (10¼-inch) skillet but a 26 cm (10¼-inch) buffet casserole would also be suitable.

FOR THE PASTRY:

225 g (8 oz) plain flour
a pinch of salt
25 g (1 oz) icing sugar
140 g (5 oz) unsalted butter, chilled and cubed
1 egg, beaten
1½–2 tablespoons cold water

FOR THE FILLING:

60 g (2 oz) unsalted butter
85 g (3 oz) caster sugar
about 1.25 kg (2 lb 12 oz) dessert apples (British Cox's or French Reinette are best), peeled, cored and cut into thick slices

1 For the pastry, sift the flour, salt and sugar into a food processor, add the butter and process briefly, until the mixture resembles breadcrumbs. Add the egg and enough water to form a fairly moist dough. Gather the dough together with your hands and wrap it in cling film. Chill for at least an hour.

2 For the filling, place your pan over a direct heat. Add the butter, reduce the heat to low and melt the butter and then add about two-thirds of the caster sugar. Stirring constantly, cook for 3–5 minutes or until it is golden brown: do not leave it much longer or it will burn.

3 Remove from the heat. Place the apples on top of the caramelised sugar, side by side.

4 Preheat the oven to Gas Mark 5/190°C/375°F. Bring the pastry back to room temperature and roll it out to a circle about 5 cm (2 inches) larger than the pan. Place this over the apples and carefully tuck in the edges, between the fruit and the pan: this forms the tart's sides, once it has been inverted.

5 Prick the pastry a couple of times and then bake for 30–35 minutes, until it is golden brown.

6 Remove from the oven and allow to cool for at least 10 minutes. Run a knife around the edges of the pan, place the serving plate on top and then carefully – but swiftly – turn it over, so the tart inverts on to the serving plate. Serve warm, with crème fraîche.

TARTE AUX PRUNEAUX

Serves 6 Freezing not recommended
Preparation time: 2 hours soaking + 20 minutes + 30 minutes baking

This is such an easy tart to do, as the pastry and filling are all one – a type of frangipane mixture of ground almonds, flour, butter and sugar, with some egg whites to lighten it. There is added flavouring from the prunes, which have been soaked in Armagnac. Try to use either Agen prunes or large Californian ones.

Serve in wedges while still warm, with a dollop of crème fraîche.

200 g (7 oz) large prunes
3 tablespoons Armagnac
100 g (3½ oz) unsalted butter, melted
100 g (3½ oz) ground almonds
50 g (1¾ oz) plain flour
150 g (5½ oz) icing sugar
2 large egg whites

1 First, soak the prunes in the Armagnac for about 2 hours or until they have plumped up a little. Remove the stones. Preheat the oven to Gas Mark 5/190°C/375°F.
2 Pour the melted butter into a bowl, add the ground almonds and sift in the flour and sugar. Add a tablespoon of the Armagnac from the prune dish and combine well.
3 Whisk the egg whites until stiff and then gradually fold them into the mixture. (It will not look very promising at this stage: do not panic, it will shape up nicely in the oven!)
4 Butter a 22 cm (8½-inch), round gratin dish or a 24 cm (9½-inch), oval gratin dish. Spoon in the frangipane mixture and level off the surface. Top with the prunes, in a neat circle. Press them down a little into the mixture.
5 Bake for 15 minutes and then reduce the oven heat to Gas Mark 4/180°C/350°F and continue to cook for 12–15 minutes or until the filling has puffed up and is golden brown. (A skewer inserted into the middle should come out clean.)
6 Remove and leave to cool for at least 20–30 minutes before serving – straight from the dish – in wedges, with some crème fraîche.

TARTE AU CHOCOLAT

Serves 8–10 Freezing not recommended

Preparation time: making + chilling pastry + 20 minutes baking + 2 hours setting

This is a chocolate lover's dream: a rich, creamy chocolate filling in a crisp short pastry. The tart should be eaten on the day it is made, otherwise it might become soggy. Be sure to use chocolate with a high percentage of cocoa solids: I recommend using one with 55–70 per cent.

You can ring the changes with the filling by adding some finely chopped crystallised ginger or dried pears to the base before topping with the chocolate cream.

1 quantity of sweet shortcrust pastry (page 63)

400 ml (14 fl oz) double cream

300 g (10½ oz) dark chocolate (minimum 55% cocoa solids), chopped

1 tablespoon brandy

1 Roll out the pastry to fit a 28 cm (11-inch), oval gratin dish or a 24 cm (9½-inch), deep, loose-bottomed tart tin. Prick all over and chill for at least 2 hours or, preferably, overnight.

2 Preheat the oven to Gas Mark 5/190°C/375°F. Line the tart with foil or greaseproof paper and fill with baking beans. Bake blind for 20 minutes. Remove the foil and beans and continue to cook for another 10 minutes or until the pastry is cooked and is a light golden brown.

3 Place the cream in a heavy saucepan and bring slowly to the boil. Immediately the bubbles appear, remove from the heat and stir in the chopped chocolate. Stir (or whisk) until smooth. Stir in the brandy and allow to cool for about 20 minutes.

4 Pour into the cooled pastry case. Leave for about 2 hours, to cool and set, before cutting into thin slices.

BISCUITS & SPECIAL OCCASION CAKES

Here is a collection of biscuits and special occasion cakes. Apart from the Gâteau St Honoré , they are all really easy to make. As with all the other recipes in this book, the key to success is to use good-quality ingredients.

Gâteau St Honoré is, indeed, rather complicated, but I can assure you that the results are sensational. It not only looks impressive, it tastes divine. The same applies to the Strawberry mille-feuille, which makes a fantastic dessert. Galettes au fromage are delicately cheesy biscuits that would be a welcome change from sausage rolls with pre-dinner drinks. Tuiles aux amandes and Petits Gâteaux Basques are traditional classics, instantly evoking thoughts of the treasure-trove that awaits you in France's wonderful pâtisseries.

Biscuits, generally, should be taken out of the oven while they are still slightly soft: they will become crisp as they cool on a wire rack.

GALETTES AU FROMAGE

Makes 20–22   Freezing recommended
Preparation time: 20 minutes + 15 minutes baking

These little biscuits – which are good to serve with drinks – are light, buttery and crisp. Although most French recipes stipulate the use of grated gruyère cheese in their galettes, I find the result rather too over-powering. Using grated Parmesan, you still have an obviously cheesy bite but without any lingering smelly cheese taste!

225 g (8 oz) unsalted butter, softened
200 g (7 oz) plain flour, sifted
125 g (4½ oz) Parmesan cheese, grated
½ teaspoon salt

1 Preheat the oven to Gas Mark 2/150°C/300°F. In a mixing bowl, work the butter with a wooden spoon, until smooth and soft. Then add the remaining ingredients and combine thoroughly but not too vigorously.

2 Once well combined, flour your hands and then shape the dough into a ball. Place on a floured board and roll out to a thickness of about 1 cm (½ inch). Using a 5 cm (2-inch) pastry cutter, cut out little rounds of the dough and place on a pizza tray or one large or two small lightly buttered baking sheets. Using a fork, prick each galette a couple of times.

3 Bake for 10 minutes. Increase the oven heat to Gas Mark 6/200°C/400°F. Bake for a further 5–6 minutes, until pale golden brown at the edges.

4 Remove and leave to cool for 2 minutes. Then using a spatula, carefully remove to a wire rack to become cold. Take care doing this as they are fairly fragile.

TUILES AUX AMANDES

Makes about 12 Freezing recommended
Preparation time: 5 minutes + 5–6 minutes baking

Provided that you follow a couple of rules about making *tuiles*, you should end up with the crispest, crunchiest biscuit in an old-fashioned tile shape. Firstly, butter the baking sheets thoroughly, otherwise you will have difficulty removing the *tuiles* while hot. Secondly, shape them, over the rolling pin immediately they are removed from the baking sheet, for the best *tuile* (tile) shape.

25 g (1 oz) unsalted butter
50 g (1¾ oz) icing sugar
25 g (1 oz) plain flour
1 large egg white
25 g (1 oz) flaked almonds
sifted icing sugar, to serve

1 Preheat the oven to Gas Mark 6/200°C/400°F. Melt the butter and pour it into a mixing bowl. Sift in the sugar and flour. Add the egg white and, using a balloon whisk, whisk until the mixture is smooth.

2 Drop about 12 spoonfuls on to two well buttered baking sheets. Ensure that they are well spaced out. With the back of a spoon, spread out the mixture, until you have 12 thin circles. Sprinkle the tops with the flaked almonds.

3 Bake for 5–6 minutes, until the edges are a light golden brown.

4 Remove and quickly lift off each one – with a broad palette knife or spatula – and drape over a rolling pin (or clean bottle), to form the *tuile* shape. Leave to cool. Sprinkle with icing sugar to serve.

PETITS GÂTEAUX BASQUES

Makes 4; serves 8 Freezing recommended
Preparation time: 10 minutes + chilling + 30 minutes baking

Gâteau basque was the local speciality when I lived in the French Pyrenees, working as an *assistante* in a *lycée*. Although large ones were for sale in all the pâtisseries, it was the small cakes – *petits gâteaux basques* – which I remember most fondly. I used to meet my friend Mary-An, who was an *assistante* some 30 km away, every Wednesday afternoon in Pau, which was equidistant from both our towns. Poor as we were, we used to treat ourselves to a cup of coffee or tea and a little cake in a rather chic café. During the summer months, we ordered *tartes aux fraises*, but during the long winter months, it was these individual *gâteaux basques*, little cakes of short, lemony pastry enclosing a vanilla-infused crème pâtissière. Made in egg plates they are large enough to serve two but you could make individual ones in 12 cm (4½-inch), loose-bottomed, metal tartlet tins, using about 8 tablespoons (about two-thirds of the recipe quantity) of crème pâtissière.

300 g (10½ oz) self-raising flour, sifted
50 g (1¾ oz) fine semolina
150 g (5½ oz) unsalted butter, chilled and cubed
150 g (5½ oz) caster sugar
grated zest of 1 lemon
2 eggs, beaten
1 tablespoon lemon juice
2 quantities of crème pâtissière (page 63)
icing sugar, sifted, to decorate

1 First make the pastry: place the flour, semolina, butter, sugar and lemon zest in a food processor. Whizz briefly to combine.

2 Mix together the eggs and lemon juice; then slowly pour this into the processor, with the machine running. Gather together the dough with your hands and wrap it in cling film. Chill for at least an hour.

3 Divide the dough into four, then carefully roll out to about twice the size of the egg plates. Place these carefully into the plates. Push the pastry gently into the edges, but leave the 'overhang', to make the top.

4 Spoon 3 tablespoons of the crème pâtissière into each plate. Very carefully flip back the overhang and gently press into place, to make the tops. Patch it up carefully, so all the crème pâtissière is covered. Don't worry if it looks rather messy – it will even out slightly as it bakes. Chill for 1–2 hours or, preferably, overnight.

5 Preheat the oven to Gas Mark 4/180°C/350°F. Bake for about 30 minutes or until golden brown. Remove to a wire rack to cool completely before decanting. Dust lightly with icing sugar before serving.

STRAWBERRY MILLE-FEUILLES

Serves 6–8 Freezing not recommended
Preparation time: 15 minutes + 12 minutes baking + 2 hours chilling

Instead of whipped cream or *crème chantilly*, I like to fill mille-feuilles with a mixture of mascarpone cream cheese, sweetened with a little crème pâtissière. The strawberries are first macerated in a little balsamic vinegar, which really enhances the sweetness of the berries.

375 g (13 oz) packet of 'ready-rolled' puff pastry
icing sugar
250 g (9 oz) strawberries
½ tablespoon balsamic vinegar
25 g (1 oz) caster sugar
2 tablespoons crème pâtissière (page 63)
250 g (9 oz) mascarpone cream cheese

1 Preheat the oven to Gas Mark 7/220°C/425°F. First cut the puff pastry into two rectangles about 23 cm (9 inches) by 10 cm (4 inches). Place these on a large baking sheet and prick them all over: it is very important to prick evenly over the entire surface, otherwise the pastry will rise too much.

2 Bake for 12 minutes or until puffed up and golden brown on top.

3 Remove the rectangles at once to a wire rack and sprinkle about ½ tablespoon of sifted icing sugar over the top of each, as evenly as possible. Once completely cold, very carefully cut the sheets in half lengthways, using an extremely sharp knife.

4 For the filling, hull and slice the strawberries and place in a bowl, with the balsamic vinegar and sugar. Stir and leave for 20 minutes.

5 Whisk together the crème pâtissière and mascarpone and then add the strawberries. Place this in the fridge for 1–2 hours, to firm up a little.

6 To assemble, place one rectangle of pastry on a large serving plate. (Be sure to use your most beautiful-looking sheet for the top!) Carefully spread with one-third of the strawberry mixture, top with another pastry sheet, then more cream, another pastry sheet, more cream and then finally top with the last pastry sheet. Cut into slices with a very sharp knife to serve.

GÂTEAU ST HONORÉ

Serves 8 Freezing not recommended
Preparation time: making pastry + chilling + 1 hour

In Edinburgh there is a wonderful French baker called Bertrand Espouy. His bakery, 'The Auld Alliance', produces the best sourdough bread, croissants and baguettes in Scotland. For special occasions, I ask him to make his famous Gâteau St Honoré, which cannot be bettered.

Although Bertrand makes his base with *pâte sucrée*, I have substituted a puff pastry base, for speed. Some recipes fill the gâteau simply with a *crème chantilly* and *crème pâtissière* mixture but Bertrand's *crème chiboust* makes the filling even more special. *Crème chiboust* is a light cream made of hot *crème pâtissière* mixed with Italian meringue, which is made by pouring a boiling sugar syrup over the whisked egg whites. It can be stiffened slightly by adding a couple of leaves of gelatine but I prefer not to do this: I like a soft filling, not a firm, jellied one. Chiboust was the name of a French pâtissier who invented this version of the gâteau St Honoré, naming it after the fashionable street in Paris where his shop was located.

The quality of the choux pastry is, obviously, crucial to the success of the gâteau. Many people are a little in awe of making choux pastry but the retained heat of a cast-iron saucepan is really helpful here: the heat helps to cook the egg as it is added to the paste, stopping the mixture from becoming too soft and sticky. The result is perfectly light and crisp.

FOR THE BASE AND CHOUX BUNS:
25 cm (10-inch) circle of puff pastry, cooked
65 g (2½ oz) plain flour
50 g (1¾ oz) unsalted butter, diced
1 teaspoon caster sugar
¼ teaspoon salt
150 ml (¼ pint) cold water
2 large eggs, beaten

FOR THE CRÈME CHIBOUST:
½ vanilla pod
1 quantity of crème pâtissière, hot (page 63)
360 g (12¼ oz) caster sugar
30 g (1¼ oz) liquid glucose
80 ml (3 fl oz) water
6 egg whites
a pinch of salt

FOR THE CARAMEL:
100 g (3½ oz) caster sugar
50 ml (2 fl oz) cold water

1 Preheat the oven to Gas Mark 6/200°C/400°F. Place the freshly cooked puff pastry base on a large serving platter.

2 For the choux buns, sift the flour on to a sheet of greaseproof paper. Place the butter in a medium-sized, heavy-based saucepan, with the sugar, salt and water. Slowly bring to the boil. Once it has reached a rolling boil, remove from the heat, quickly tip in the flour all at once and beat vigorously with a wooden spoon.

3 Cook over a low heat for 2 minutes, beating

constantly, until the mixture forms a smooth ball, leaving the sides of the pan. Remove from the heat and add the eggs, one at a time, beating thoroughly. You may not need all the egg. Continue beating well for another 2–3 minutes.

4 Now either pipe or spoon about 25 small buns with the choux mixture on to a buttered pizza tray or baking tray. Be sure to space well apart as they will expand during cooking.

5 Bake for about 25–30 minutes or until golden brown and crisp. Remove to a wire tray and immediately pierce each bun underneath with a skewer, to release the steam. Leave to cool.

6 Meanwhile, make the *crème chiboust*. Split the vanilla pod and scrape out the seeds. Mix these into the hot *crème pâtissière*. Keep it hot while you make the Italian meringue: place the sugar, glucose and water in a saucepan and bring very slowly to the boil, taking great care that the sugar dissolves well. When it boils, brush the sides of the pan with a brush soaked in cold water, so the sugar does not burn. Check the temperature with a sugar thermometer.

7 Whisk the egg whites with a pinch of salt until stiff, but not dry. When the syrup has reached 121°C on the thermometer, pour the syrup carefully over the egg whites, whisking at the same time, until the meringue is very firm.

8 Incorporate a third of the meringue in the hot *crème pâtissière* with a whisk and then fold in the rest carefully with a spatula.

9 Make the caramel: heat the sugar in a heavy-based saucepan, with the water, stirring constantly. Boil for about 5 minutes or until a pale golden colour. (During this time, again, brush down the sides of the pan with a pastry brush.) Stop cooking when the caramel is a pale amber colour. Using tongs, carefully dip the choux buns into the caramel to glaze the tops.

10 Once the caramel has hardened, pipe some of the *crème chiboust* into the choux buns. Place about 16 of these buns around the edge of the pastry base (the remaining buns can be used as profiteroles). Then using a piping bag – or a spoon – fill the centre of the gâteau with the *crème chiboust*. This gâteau should be eaten on the day it is made.

CRÈME PÂTISSIÈRE

Makes about 450 ml (¾ pint)
Freezing not recommended
Preparation and cooking time: 6–7 minutes

Although there are many different methods of making *crème pâtissière*, this is mine: it is incredibly easy.

2 egg yolks
60 g (2 oz) caster sugar
25 g (1 oz) plain flour, sifted
300 ml (½ pint) full-fat milk
1 teaspoon pure vanilla extract

1 In a bowl, mix together the egg yolks and sugar. Then sift in the flour and mash together to combine thoroughly.
2 In a heavy-based saucepan, bring the milk slowly to the boil. As soon as you see bubbles, remove from the heat and pour about one-third over the egg mixture, stirring continuously. Pour this mixture back into the pan and cook slowly, whisking all the time for 3–4 minutes, until thickened and smooth. Be sure to cook sufficiently or it will taste of raw flour.
3 Remove from the heat and stir in the vanilla. Pour into a bowl and cover closely with cling film, to prevent a skin from forming. Use when completely cold.

SWEET SHORTCRUST PASTRY

Makes about 450 g (1 lb)
Freezing recommended
Preparation time: 3 minutes + chilling

Although the classic sweet pastries – *pâte brisée, pâte sucrée* and *pâte sablée* – are made by hand (the butter worked into the flour, then sugar, and eggs added), I confess I always use my food processor, for a couple of reasons. The main reason is speed: it takes no longer than 3 minutes. Also, since I keep my butter in the fridge, I can make pastry immediately I have the urge, instead of having to wait until the butter has softened slightly, which, in my Scottish kitchen, can take some time.

225 g (8 oz) plain flour
a pinch of salt
25 g (1 oz) icing sugar
140 g (5 oz) unsalted butter, chilled and diced
1 egg
about 1½ tablespoons cold water

1 Sift the flour, salt and sugar into a food processor. Add the diced butter and process briefly, until the mixture resembles breadcrumbs.
2 Whisk together the egg and the water and slowly add them, while the machine is running. Stop and check: the mixture should now look fairly moist, not a mass of dry crumbs but it will not necessarily have clumped together into a ball. You may need to add a little more water. Tip the mixture into a bowl and gather it with your hands into a ball. Wrap in cling film and chill for at least an hour before rolling out.

INDEX